The colonists' ship, the Ann, made landfall on January 13, 1733 nea[r] Charleston, SC. From there, the colonists sailed south to an area aroun[d] Port Royal, SC where they waited for Oglethorpe to go ahead with a sma[ll] group to scout out the site of the new colony. He chose the location of what is now Downtown Savannah for several reasons. It was high ground which could be easily defended and the river bluff allowed large ships to draft close to the bank. The river also provided a source of fresh water. In addition, the Yamacraw Indians, being familiar with the land, had chosen it as the site of their village. Fortunately, the Indians, led by Tomochichi, were friendly and open to the colonists settling on the bluff. Oglethorpe returned to get the colonists and the entire group arrived on the bluff on February 12, 1733.

STATUE OF GENERAL OGLETHORPE ▶

With the help of William Bull, a civil engineer from Charleston, Oglethorpe proceeded to lay out the new town. No one knows for sure where or how Oglethorpe came up with the plan for Savannah, but there is little doubt that his design directly influenced the unique environment that has grown up around it. The basic component of his plan was a ward. It was comprised of 8 blocks. The larger four blocks are called tything blocks which are further subdivided by east-west lanes. The four smaller blocks that front the squares are known as trust lots. The plan intended the tything blocks to be used for residential purposes while the trust lots would serve as the sites of civic and commercial structures. The city could be expanded by simply replicating the pattern.

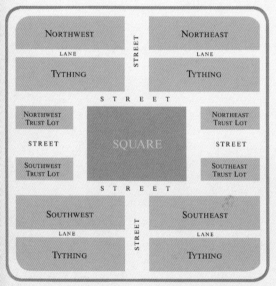

▲ **TYPICAL WARD**

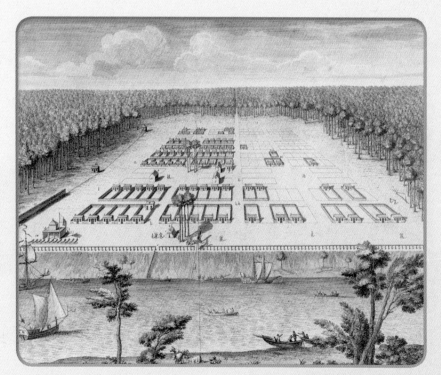

▲ **VIEW OF SAVANNAH IN 1734**

The original plan called for 4 squares (now known as Johnson, Wright, Ellis and Telfair). By 1851, the city had grown to include 24 squares. Today 22 squares remain including Ellis, which reopened in 2010.

During the Revolutionary War, the British took control of Savannah in 1778. In 1779, a large French and American force attempted to take the city by siege and later by direct assault (The Siege of Savannah) but they failed. The British retained control of Savannah until the Americans ultimately won the war.

With American Independence secured, Savannah and its economy blossomed. The soil and climate were found to be particularly favorable for the production of rice and cotton. However, picking out lint and cotton seeds manually was a labor intensive process which limited cotton's viability as a revenue generator. In 1793, Eli Whitney invented the cotton gin which mechanically separated the seeds from cotton. His invention allowed land and plantation owners to make huge profits growing cotton for export to England. The port of Savannah and the shipping merchants also benefited from this economic boom. It was during this antebellum period that many of the great mansions, public buildings and churches of Savannah were constructed. Massive fires in 1796 and 1820 each wiped out half of the town and a yellow fever outbreak in 1820 killed a tenth of the population but Savannah was resilient. It became known as one of the most picturesque cities in America populated by a unique and cultured citizenry. Then, the Civil War began.

In 1862, Fort Pulaski was captured by Union forces and held through the remainder of the war. Possession of the fort allowed the Union to impose a sea blockade that crippled the city and its economy. The Union General William Sherman took Savannah with little effort on December 21, 1864. His forces had burned and destroyed everything they encountered on their March to the Sea from Atlanta but Sherman was awed by Savannah's beauty and chose not to destroy it. Instead he presented it to President Lincoln as a Christmas gift.

PULASKI MONUMENT

NAVAL STORES

CONFEDERATE MONUMENT

After the war, reconstruction efforts began. It was a slow process but by the turn of the century Savannah's economy was strong again. Cotton led the way and Savannah also became a leader in exporting lumber and naval stores (products such as resin related to the construction and maintenance of wooden ships). Economic troubles would visit Savannah again in the early 1900s in the form of the boll weevil, which ravaged cotton production in the Southeast, and the advent of metal ships. Savannah would not right itself again until the 1950's when a broader based economy took hold.

It was also during this time that a group of civic-minded women formed the Historic Savannah Foundation, which is credited with beginning the movement to save Savannah's historic structures. They had been spurred to action by witnessing the loss of several of the city's architectural treasures. In 1966, the Savannah Historic District was declared a National Historic Landmark. Fortunately, the great significance of Savannah's past was recognized and protected early enough to preserve its charm for future generations.

ALONG THE RIVERFRONT

SAVANNAH RIVER

RIVER STREET

RIVER STREET

EMMET PARK

BAY STREET

WASHINGTON SQUARE

WARREN SQUARE

REYNOLDS SQUARE

JOHNSON SQUARE

BRYAN STREET

ST. JULIAN ST.

CONGRESS STREET

BRYAN STREET

ST. JULIAN ST.

CONGRESS STREET

HABERSHAM STREET

HOUSTON STREET

LINCOLN STREET

ABERCORN ST.

DRAYTON STREET

BULL STREET

WHITAKER STREET

EAST BROAD STREET

PRICE ST.

BROUGHTON STREET

STATE STREET

Walking time: approx. 45 minutes • Walking distance: approx. 1.2 miles

TOUR 1

1 OGLETHORPE'S BENCH- Tour 1 begins where the recorded history of Savannah started. This bench marks the approximate location of Oglethorpe's tent where he spent his first night in Georgia while scouting out potential sites for the colony. It also marks the landing site of the first colonists which took place about a week after Oglethorpe's original scouting visit

This photo (c1909) shows the buildings near ► Oglethorpe's Bench that were demolished to make way for the Hyatt Hotel. Many Savannahians were upset when the modern looking Hyatt Hotel was constructed. The hotel's architecture did not fit at all with the historic nature of downtown and its backside bisected River Street. Legal battles were waged in an attempt to stop the project but the developers ultimately prevailed.

OGLETHORPE'S BENCH

WALK EAST ON BAY STREET FOR LOCATIONS 2-10.

2 CITY HALL (c1905) The interior of this public building features an impressive rotunda 30 feet wide and rising 70 feet high to a beautiful stained glass dome. The exterior of the dome is gilded with a thin layer of 23kt gold. City Hall occupies the former site of the City Exchange.

◄ **CITY EXCHANGE (c1799)** This building served both public and private interests until it was acquired by the city in 1812. It was demolished in 1904 to make way for City Hall. A small replica of the City Exchange tower and its fire bell can be seen a few hundred feet east on Bay Street (see **8**).

3 US CUSTOM HOUSE (c1852) The granite used in the construction of this substantial all stone building was shipped from a quarry in Quincy, Massachusetts. It is notable for its six monolithic columns which weigh 15 tons apiece. A plaque recognizes that this building occupies the site of Oglethorpe's former wood frame residence and headquarters. It was also the site of the city's first public building which stood on the rear of the lot where John Wesley preached one of his first sermons in America in 1736.

4 WASHINGTON'S GUNS- These guns known locally as "George and Martha" were captured from the British at the Battle of Yorktown. They were presented to the Chatham Artillery (see **1**) by President George Washington during his visit to Savannah in 1791 in appreciation of their service.

◄ From your vantage point at Washington's Guns, look back to the west at the intersection of Bay and Bull Streets. This sketch shows General Sherman's Union Army entering Savannah on December 21, 1864.

Sherman's massive force of 62,000 men was able to take Savannah without a fight because the Confederate Army, about 10,000 men, had used pontoon bridges to retreat into South Carolina during the night of December 20, 1864. This decision to retreat saved Savannah from certain destruction. ▼

THE SAVANNAH COTTON EXCHANGE (c1887)

This building is currently the home of Solomon's Masonic Lodge Number One. It was originally constructed to house the Cotton Exchange to further the interests of cotton merchants. At the time, Savannah and Liverpool, England were the only two places in the world where the price of cotton was quoted. It was the first building in America to incorporate "air rights" as it was constructed over the Drayton Street ramp that descends to the river. This fact can be seen more readily from River Street. The original terra cotta griffon fountain (c 1889-seen in photo) in front of the Exchange was destroyed by a spectacular single car crash in 2008. It was painstakingly reconstructed over 10 months to form a mold for the new concrete replica that was rededicated in December 2009. A griffon is a mythological beast that served to guard ancient treasure. The griffon fountain is surrounded by elaborate ironwork featuring profiles of famous statesmen and poets. This ironwork was originally located at the Barclay-Wetter House (see ⑦) .

▲ Sampling Cotton in the 1890's

⑥ FACTOR'S ROW AND FACTOR'S WALK-

This collection of buildings that appear to be two to three stories tall from Bay Street are really five to six story buildings that have their first floors on River Street. Now occupied with a mix of retail stores, restaurants, offices and residential units, these buildings used to be the Wall Street of Savannah when cotton was king. Named for the cotton factors (or brokers), the upper levels of these buildings served as offices. The lower levels served as warehouses for cotton and naval stores that were loaded and unloaded from ships docked along River Street. From the bridges and walkways over Factor's Walk, one can see the cobblestones that were used to pave streets and build retaining walls on the sandy bluff. These cobblestones were used as ballast in sailing ships which was left in Savannah after taking on a load of cotton or other exports.

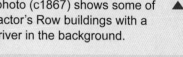

This photo (c1867) shows some of the Factor's Row buildings with a busy river in the background. ▲

⑦ SAVANNAH AREA CHAMBER OF COMMERCE AND CONVENTION AND VISITORS BUREAU

(c1912) Now housing the executive offices of the Chamber of Commerce and Visitors Bureau, this granite building was originally built for the Hibernia Bank. You can stop in here for information, maps and brochures.

◀ This site and several of the adjacent buildings were previously occupied by the imposing and architecturally diverse BOARD OF TRADE BUILDING (c1875) which was the successor of the Savannah Naval Stores Exchange.

TOUR
1

CONTINUED..

8 **CITY EXCHANGE FIRE BELL-** This is a small replica of the City Exchange bell tower. The fire bell hanging in this replica tower was imported from Amsterdam and dates from 1802. It originally hung in the City Exchange (see **2**) tower which was manned every night due to the ever present threat of fires.

City Exchange, 18??

9 **EMMET PARK-** This park is named for the Irish Patriot Robert Emmet who was hanged by the British after leading an uprising in Dublin intended to gain Irish independence. This park is a special place for those of Irish descent and the Celtic Cross ceremony is held at the Celtic Cross monument each year on the Sunday prior to St. Patrick's Day. As you pass through Emmet Park, you will pass by the following monuments: the Georgia Hussars Marker, the Salzburger Monument, US Marine Corp Reserve Monument, the Celtic Cross, Vietnam Memorial, Chatham Artillery Monument, GA Medical Society Monument to Dr. Noble Jones.

10 **OLD HARBOR LIGHT (c1858)** This beacon light was constructed by the U.S. Government to guide ships past the hulls of sunken ships in the channel. The British sunk these ships in 1779 in an attempt to prevent the French navy (allies of the Americans in the Revolutionary War) from entering Savannah. The large anchors displayed around the light are remnants of historic ships that have been discovered over the years by dredging activity in the Savannah River shipping channel.

  USE CROSSWALK TO CROSS BAY ST. AND WALK SOUTH DOWN EAST BROAD STREET

11 **TRUSTEES' GARDEN-** This area (about 10 acres) was set aside by the Trustees in 1733 and served as an experimental farm where different crops were tested for their potential in the new colony. Some of the crops included peaches, rice, cotton, grapes, flax, hemp, indigo, olives, and mulberry trees for silk production. One of the early promises to England was that the colony of Georgia would be a significant source of silk, a sought after commodity at the time. However, silk was not a successful crop in Georgia and the garden was closed and subdivided in 1755.

12 **THE PIRATES' HOUSE (c1754)** Now a favorite restaurant, this building was originally a seaman's tavern in the days of sailing ships and pirates. It is rumored that an underground tunnel connected the rum cellar to the river where drunken men were placed aboard ships to later awake at sea as unwitting crew members. Robert Louis Stevenson's Treasure Island was said to be inspired by events that occurred here. Captain Flint, the infamous blue-faced pirate from the book, supposedly died here in an upstairs room and is rumored to haunt the place on moonless nights.

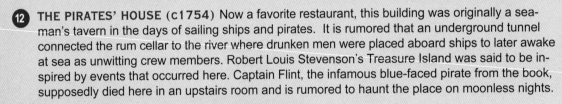

13 **THE HERB HOUSE (c1734)**
This home is considered the oldest surviving home in Georgia. It originally served as a home for the gardener of Trustees' Garden. When the garden failed, the Herb House was expanded into a seaman's tavern which later became The Pirates' House.

TURN AROUND AND WALK NORTH BACK TO BAY STREET. USE CROSSWALK TO CROSS BAY STREET. TO GET DOWN TO RIVER STREET YOU MAY USE A TREACHEROUS SET OF STAIRS OR USE THE DESCENDING SIDEWALK AROUND THE GA POWER BUILDING. WALK WEST ON RIVER STREET.

14 FORT WAYNE- This fort, originally known as Fort Savannah, was constructed in 1762 on the site of Trustees' Garden. Some of the original brick walls of the fort can be seen from General McIntosh Blvd. (the extension of Bay Street past East Broad Street). During the Revolutionary War, the poorly prepared Americans used this fort to defend against the British attack in 1778. The British prevailed and held Savannah as a base of operations in the south for the remainder of the war. After the war ended, the fort was renamed in honor of General "Mad Anthony" Wayne, a battle-hardened American general. Wayne led the final "mop up" of the British in the south after the back-breaking American victory at Yorktown.

▲ GENERAL "MAD ANTHONY" WAYNE

15 OLYMPIC YACHTING CAULDRON- This cauldron was lit by the Olympic Flame from Mt. Olympus at the Savannah Opening Ceremony on July 20, 1996. The six sails represent the Olympic yachting events that were held off the coast of Savannah during the 1996 Olympic Games.

17 ROUSAKIS PLAZA- In 1973 the city began a visionary project to convert River Street from a ramshackle collection of rotten shipping wharfs into the pedestrian friendly area that you are experiencing today. It is thought to be the finest reclamation and restoration of a true antebellum shipping port in the United States. Rousakis Plaza is named in honor of Mayor John Rousakis who served as Savannah's mayor for 21 years beginning in 1970. The plaza encompasses all of the bricked areas along the riverfront.

RIVER STREET IN THE EARLY 1900s.

16 THE WAVING GIRL STATUE (ERECTED 1972)

Florence Martus (1868-1943) became known as "The Waving Girl" by sailors around the world. She spent most of her life on Elba Island (this island can be seen by walking further east on River Street and looking for the large natural gas tanks that are downriver). From the porch of her home on Elba Island, she waved a handkerchief by day and a lantern by night at ships entering or leaving the port of Savannah. It is said that she never missed waving at a single ship between 1887 and 1931 when she moved into town.

This photo from 1892 shows what one would have seen along the river banks during this period. At that time Savannah was one of the leading Naval Stores markets in the world. Naval Stores, the generic term for products derived from pine trees such as turpentine, pitch and rosin used in wooden ship construction, shared the acres of docks and storage yards alongside cotton.
▼

▲ FLORENCE MARTUS, THE WAVING GIRL (PHOTO c1933)

TOUR 1

CONTINUED..

18 **THE ECHO CHAMBER-** As you make your way westward along River Street, keep an eye out for the Bob's Your Uncle/Life is Good store. Directly across the street from this store, you will find a curious spot known as the Echo Chamber. Most Savannahians don't even know about this little secret. X marks the spot where you should stand and make a little noise. A yell or a whisper is equally effective but be careful how silly you act because only the person on the X can hear the mysterious echoes.

19 **THE SAVANNAH COTTON EXCHANGE (c1887)** Viewed from River Street, one can appreciate the concept of "air rights" that was utilized in the construction of this building.

20 **RIVER STREET SWEETS-** Established in 1973, this is Savannah's oldest candy store. It is the best place in town to indulge a sweet tooth. Stop in and sample a world famous praline or try my favorite, a delicious dark chocolate bear claw.

21 **THE AFRICAN AMERICAN MONUMENT (ERECTED 2002)** This bronze monument displays an African American family embracing with broken shackles on their feet. The monument features an inscription by poet Maya Angelou. This monument commemorates and honors the contributions of African Americans to the cultural, social, educational, economic and spiritual life of Savannah.

22 **VISITORS INFORMATION CENTER-** This is a good place to get information or use the public restroom facilities.

USE THE ELEVATOR AT LOCATION 22 TO GO BACK UP TO BAY STREET. THIS IS THE END OF TOUR 1.

TOUR 2 — THE FIRST SQUARES

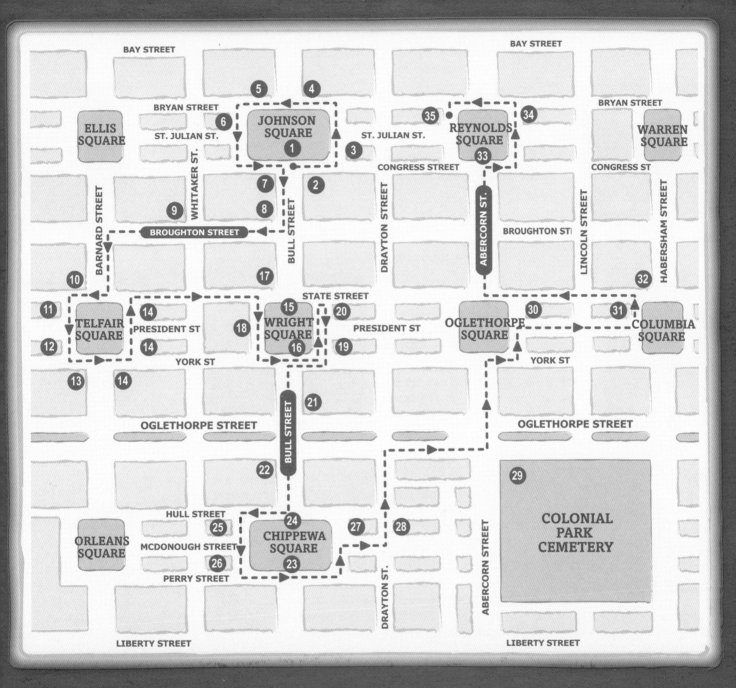

BAY STREET

BRYAN STREET

ST. JULIAN ST.

ELLIS SQUARE

JOHNSON SQUARE

5 4

6

1

3

7 2

8

9

BROUGHTON STREET

BULL STREET

WHITAKER ST.

BARNARD STREET

17

10

11

TELFAIR SQUARE

14

PRESIDENT ST

12

14

13 14

STATE STREET

15 **WRIGHT SQUARE** 20

18

16 19

YORK ST.

BULL STREET

21

OGLETHORPE STREET

22

HULL STREET

25

MCDONOUGH STREET

ORLEANS SQUARE

24 **CHIPPEWA SQUARE**

26 23

PERRY STREET

LIBERTY STREET

BAY STREET

BRYAN STREET

35 **REYNOLDS SQUARE** 34

33

CONGRESS STREET

DRAYTON STREET

ABERCORN ST.

BROUGHTON ST

30 **OGLETHORPE SQUARE**

PRESIDENT ST

LINCOLN STREET

WARREN SQUARE

CONGRESS ST

HABERSHAM STREET

32

31 **COLUMBIA SQUARE**

YORK ST

OGLETHORPE STREET

29 **COLONIAL PARK CEMETERY**

27 28

DRAYTON ST.

ABERCORN STREET

LIBERTY STREET

Walking time: approx. 1 hour & 15 minutes • Walking distance: approx. 1.7 miles

TOUR 2

JOHNSON SQUARE- This square was the first square laid out by Oglethorpe and was named in honor of Governor Robert Johnson of South Carolina, a friend of Oglethorpe's who provided assistance and supplies to Savannah in its earliest days. This square has historically been a center of commercial and civic activities. In the early years, the lots surrounding this square contained the public store in addition to the public grist mill and oven where the colonists obtained their bread. The Declaration of Independence was publicly read in this square on August 10, 1776 and was celebrated riotously.

1 NATHANAEL GREENE MONUMENT (COMPLETED 1830)
This 50 foot marble monument, intended to resemble a Roman sword, is the grave of Nathanael Greene (and his son, George Washington Greene). A personal friend of President George Washington, Greene served as the leader of the American forces in the South during the Revolutionary War. His list of battles is too long to list here but his leadership was instrumental in defeating the British.

PORTRAIT OF NATHANAEL GREENE ▶

2 THE MANGER BUILDING (c1923)
This building was originally the Savannah Hotel which was later converted to an office building. It replaced The Screven House Hotel.

THE SCREVEN HOUSE HOTEL (c1854)
This hotel was erected on the former site of Mrs. Platt's boarding house. ▶

3 CHRIST CHURCH- Founded in 1733, this church is considered the "Mother Church of Georgia." This trust lot was designated by Oglethorpe as the site of the colony's house of worship but no building was erected for some time. The current structure was erected in 1838. The two most famous rectors of Christ Church, John Wesley and George Whitefield, exercised their ministry out of the colony's courthouse building which was located to the rear of the US Custom House (see **3**).
John Wesley (1736-1737) started the first Sunday School in America there. George Whitefield (1738-1740) is considered one of the greatest evangelists of all time and one of the men responsible for the "Great Awakening."

▲
This is a drawing of the previous Christ Church building that was torn down to make way for the current structure. It was in this church building that President George Washington attended service while visiting Savannah during his southern tour of 1791.

4 JOHNSON SQUARE BUSINESS CENTER (c1911) Originally the Savannah Bank and Trust Building, this "skyscraper" avoided the fate of many of the other Johnson Square skyscrapers erected near the turn of the century.

◀ This photo from 1911 shows some of the buildings that were lost to a later addition to the Johnson Square Business Center building.

5 REGIONS BANK BUILDING- (c1957)
This building was originally built as a Morrison's cafeteria but is now occupied by a bank and offices. It was previously the site of The Pulaski House hotel. Rumor has it that a young girl in period dress named Gracie Watson is occasionally seen in the basement of this building.

Gracie Watson's grave in Bonaventure Cemetery. ▼

◄ **THE PULASKI HOUSE-** The age of the Pulaski House is unknown but it may date from as early as 1795. The hotel manager in 1864 was most eager to have General Sherman and some of his men stay here when they arrived in Savannah as a conquering army, but Sherman let him know that "we are not in the habit of paying board." The manager of the hotel in the 1880's was W.J. Watson. His only daughter, Gracie Watson, died of pneumonia in 1889 at the age of six. Her marker featuring a detailed sculpture of Gracie is the most visited grave in Bonaventure Cemetery.

6 PALMER AND CAY INSURANCE BUILDING-
Located on the northwestern trust lot, this site was originally the location of the public mill where early colonists would grind corn.

◄ Prior to the current structure, this lot was occupied by a gas station and service garage as seen in this photo from 1941.

7 SUNTRUST BANK BUILDING- This uninteresting office building and associated parking deck took the place of three elaborate "skyscrapers" that were demolished in 1975 to make way for this project.

Photo from 1929 ► showing the Whitney Hotel and Germania Bank that previously occupied this location.

◄ Another view of the Germania Bank at the corner of Congress and Bull Streets c1930.

 WALK SOUTH ON BULL STREET TO THE INTERSECTION OF BULL AND BROUGHTON STREETS.

8 SUNTRUST BANK BUILDING- PARKING DECK-
This corner was previously occupied by the dramatic Liberty Bank and Trust building.

Photo of the Liberty Bank and Trust
◄ building that was lost in 1975.

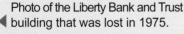

Broughton Street was the primary business district of Savannah from the 1920's through 1950's. Can you identify where today's Panera Bread is located? ▼

◄ This is a view north toward Johnson Square from Bull and Broughton Streets in the late 1800's.

TOUR 2 CONTINUED..

 TURN RIGHT AND WALK WEST ON BROUGHTON STREET TO ITS INTERSECTION WITH WHITAKER STREET.

CONTINUE WALKING WEST ON BROUGHTON STREET TO BARNARD STREET. TURN LEFT AND WALK SOUTH ON BARNARD STREET TO TELFAIR SQUARE.

9 TONDEE'S LONG ROOM- Built in 1767 at the Northwest corner of Broughton Street and Whitaker, this tavern served as a meeting place for a group of young men seeking American independence who became known as the "Liberty Boys." On June 4, 1775, instead of celebrating King George III's birthday as was tradition, the Liberty Boys raised a liberty pole to celebrate the birth of liberty. The tavern continued to serve as an important meeting place for revolutionary activities until the British occupation of Savannah in 1778. The revolutionary government of Georgia reconvened at the tavern after the war's end in 1782. Unfortunately, this birthplace of liberty in Georgia burned in the great fire of 1796.

TELFAIR SQUARE- One of the first 4 squares laid out in 1733, this square was originally named St. James' Square in honor of the royal residence in London. In early days, it was one of the most fashionable neighborhoods in Savannah. It was also the site of The Government House which served as the residence of the Royal Governors of Georgia. The square was renamed in 1883 to honor the philanthropic Telfair family.

From Telfair Square between 1872 and 1950, one would have seen the Old City Market (see 12) by looking north on Barnard Street.

10 FIRST CHATHAM BANK BUILDING- This building occupies the former location of the home of George Walton, a signer of the Declaration of Independence.

This is a photo of the home of George Walton (built between 1784 and 1790). This is where President George Washington stayed while in Savannah during his southern tour of 1791.

This site was later the location of the Odd Fellows' Hall (photo c1888).

The Odd Fellows' Hall was lost to the Fire of 1889. As seen in this photo, the Telfair Museum narrowly escaped the same fate.

11 TELFAIR ACADEMY OF ARTS AND SCIENCES- Built on the original site of The Government House (the residence of the royal governors of Georgia), this building was completed in 1819 for Alexander Telfair, the son of Governor Edward Telfair. This Regency-style mansion served as the family's home until 1875. Mary Telfair, Alexander's sister and an early patron of the arts, bequeathed the home and its furnishings to the Georgia Historical Society to be used as a museum. It is the oldest public museum in the South.

12 TRINITY UNITED METHODIST CHURCH (c1848) This church is the oldest Methodist Church in Savannah. The building is a Corinthian Greek Revival style and it resembles the design of Wesley Chapel in England.

14 THE BATHROOM TILE BUILDINGS- The three federal government buildings fronting Telfair Square were constructed in the early 1980's and are known by most locals as "The Bathroom Tile Buildings." They were a sad architectural addition to one of Savannah's finest historical squares. There were some battles over their design prior to their construction, but they somehow made it through.

13 THE JEPSON CENTER FOR THE ARTS- Designed by internationally renowned architect, Moshe Safdie, this museum opened in March 2006 and features 20th and 21st century art in addition to hosting traveling shows.

◄ This photo shows some of the unique architecture that once stood at the Southeast corner of Barnard and York streets. It is now the location of the Juliette Gordon Low Federal Building, one of the Bathroom Tile Buildings.

 WALK EAST ON STATE STREET TO WRIGHT SQUARE.

WRIGHT SQUARE- One of the first four squares, this square was laid out in 1733. It was originally named Upper Square and was also known as Percival Square. This square served as the public market until the colonial legislature relocated it to Ellis Square in 1763. In that same year, the square was renamed in honor of the last Royal Governor of Georgia, Sir James Wright.

15 GORDON MONUMENT (ERECTED 1883) This monument was placed in honor of William Washington Gordon. Gordon was one of Savannah's early mayors and he was instrumental in the expansion of the railroad system from Savannah to the interior areas of Georgia. He was the founder of the Central Railroad and Banking Company of Georgia. This monument took the place of Tomochichi's burial mound and sadly his grave is still located underneath it.

◄ This photo from the 1850's shows Tomochichi's burial mound in its original location at the center of Wright Square.

16 TOMOCHICHI'S ROCK– This stone was placed in 1899 in honor of the Yamacraw Indian chief Tomochichi. His tribe occupied the bluff where Oglethorpe and the colonists landed, but he agreed to relocate further upriver. The Indians and colonists coexisted in peace primarily due to the leadership of Tomochichi. He died on October 5, 1739 and had requested to be buried among the colonists. He was given a state funeral and Oglethorpe himself served as a pallbearer. When the Gordon Monument was placed over Tomochichi's grave, Nellie Kinzie Gordon (Gordon's daughter-in-law and mother of Juliette Gordon Low) was presumably moved by guilt and headed a group that obtained the large granite stone from a quarry in Stone Mountain,GA.

◄ This portrait of Tomochichi and his nephew Toonahowi was painted in England when they visited as guests of Oglethorpe.You might hear rumors of Tomochichi having stood over 7 feet tall. These rumors are not true. He was of "medium build."

17 CVS PHARMACY-
This corner was previously occupied by the Porter Gilmer House.

◄ **PORTER-GILMER HOUSE (c1852)**
This large residence also included unique outbuildings and gardens. It was demolished in 1916 to make way for commercial uses.

◄ This photo shows the view north on Bull St. from this location in 1915.

18 US COURTHOUSE- Originally built in 1898 as a US Post Office, this building now occupies the Northwestern and Southwestern trust lots (including what used to be President Street). It is built of Georgia marble and it originally occupied only the Southwestern trust lot and was oriented perpendicular to Wright Square.

◄ **CHATHAM ARTILLERY ARMORY (c1849)**
Originally occupying the northwestern trust lot on Wright Square, the Chatham Artillery Armory was the headquarters for the Chatham Artillery, a militia unit organized during the Revolutionary War. This unique building was demolished in 1930 to make way for the expansion of the US Courthouse.

▶ This photo shows the original footprint and orientation of the US Courthouse building toward President Street.

◄ This bird's-eye view from Wright Square viewing north in 1909 shows the US Court-house and Chatham Artillery Armory as they stood prior to the Courthouse expansion.

19 OLD CHATHAM COUNTY COURTHOUSE- This building was constructed in 1889. At the time of its completion it was considered to be one of the finest public buildings in the entire southeast. The current Courthouse building on Montgomery Street replaced this building in 1979.

▶ This photo shows the previous Chatham County Courthouse building that was constructed on the same site in 1833. During its time, its Greek Revival style matched its neighbor, the former Lutheran Church of the Ascension. (see 20)

20 LUTHERAN CHURCH OF THE ASCENSION- This congregation was organized in 1744 and the church originally constructed a wood frame structure on this site in 1756. The current gothic building was constructed between 1875 and 1879. The Lutheran Church in Savannah was founded by refugees from Salzburg, Bavaria who came to Georgia because of the colony's tolerance for persecuted Protestants. The stained glass windows in the sanctuary of this church are a spectacular sight.

The previous Lutheran church building on this site was built in 1843 ▶ in the Greek Revival style, but it was mostly demolished to make way for the current gothic structure.

  WALK SOUTH ON BULL STREET TO OGLETHORPE AVENUE.

21 WAYNE-GORDON HOUSE- JULIETTE GORDON LOW BIRTHPLACE (C1823) This home was built originally for James Wayne Moore. Moore served as the Mayor of Savannah from 1817-1819, a US Representative from Georgia from 1829-1835, and a US Supreme Court Justice for 32 years. Moore sold the home to William Washington Gordon (see 15) in 1831. Gordon's granddaughter, Juliette Gordon Low, the founder of the Girl Scouts of America, was born in this house in 1860. The Girl Scouts purchased the home in 1953 and it now serves as a museum. At the time she founded the Girl Scouts, Mrs. Low was living in the Andrew Low House (see 16 17 18).

 CONTINUE WALKING SOUTH ON BULL STREET USING THE CROSSWALK TO CROSS OVER OGLETHORPE AVE.

22 INDEPENDENT PRESBYTERIAN CHURCH- Presbyterianism was introduced to the colony by Scottish Highlanders who were imported to defend Savannah against Spanish Florida. This congregation was formed in 1755. The current structure was built in 1889-1890 and is a replica of the previous structure that burned in the fire of 1889. It is a white granite building of late Georgian colonial design. The interior is notable for its unusually high pulpit and the classic ornamentation of the vaulted ceiling. The massive steeple of this finely proportioned building is easily recognizable when viewing the skyline of Savannah.

 CONTINUE WALKING SOUTH ON BULL STREET TO CHIPPEWA SQUARE.

TOUR 2

CHIPPEWA SQUARE- Laid out in 1813, this square was named for the Battle of Chippewa where American forces had a decisive victory against the British in the War of 1812.

23 OGLETHORPE MONUMENT-
(ERECTED 1910) This bronze statue of Oglethorpe is one of Savannah's most notable monuments. The statue was designed by Daniel Chester French who is also credited with Lincoln's statue in the Lincoln Memorial in Washington, D.C. In the tradition of orienting statues of military leaders towards their enemy, General Oglethorpe is facing south to keep a watchful eye on the Spanish in Florida.

24 LOCATION OF FORREST GUMP'S BENCH- The bench where Forrest Gump (Tom Hanks) told his life story was located to the north end of this square fronting on Hull Street in-between the two crosswalks. The original bench is now located in the Savannah History Museum (see 1).

26 PHILBRICK-EASTMAN HOUSE (COMPLETED 1847)
Now housing a law firm, this fine building served as a residence for many distinguished Savannah families. It is best known for its iron fencing featuring profiles of famous poets and statesman. This ironwork is not original to this house. It is a remnant of a lost architectural treasure, the Barclay-Wetter House (see 7).

25 FIRST BAPTIST CHURCH
(c1833) This congregation organized in 1800 and moved into this classic Greek Revival architecture building when it was completed in 1833. This church is the oldest original (never burned or reconstructed) church building in Savannah.

27 SAVANNAH THEATRE-
(OPENED 1818) Originally designed by William Jay, this theatre is considered the oldest operating theatre in the United States. Very little of the original structure exists due to multiple fires and face-lifts. It was redesigned and rebuilt into its current Art Deco style as a result of a fire in 1948.

This photo shows one of the previous looks of the Savannah Theatre. ▲

 WALK EAST ON MCDONOUGH STREET TO DRAYTON STREET.

28 PARKER'S MARKET- This wonderful urban market is an excellent example of an adaptive reuse. This stop is the perfect place to take a break on the tour. Grab a drink and a snack or even a fantastic lunch. You'll be surprised by what's inside.

 TURN LEFT AND WALK NORTH ON DRAYTON STREET TO OGLETHORPE AVENUE.
TURN RIGHT AND WALK EAST ON OGLETHORPE AVENUE TO ABERCORN STREET.

TOUR 2

29 COLONIAL PARK CEMETERY- Also known as "The Old Cemetery" and "The Brick Cemetery", it was established around 1750 and was closed to further burials in 1853. Even though there are only about 600 burial markers present, it is estimated that there could be as many as 9,000 people buried here. During the Union occupation of Savannah in the Civil War, Union troops camped and stabled horses here. Many graves were desecrated during this time as some of the troops looted graves and vaults seeking valuables. They also changed the dates on some of the tombstones in a poor attempt at humor. Many of the damaged tombstones have been cemented to the cemetery's eastern wall.

◄ **BUTTON GWINNETT MEMORIAL-** One of the three Georgian signers of the Declaration of Independence, Button Gwinnett is probably the most notable person buried here. Born in England around 1735, he came to Savannah in 1765 and established himself as a general trader. His enthusiasm for colonial rights and a friendship with Dr. Lyman Hall (another GA signer) led to him being selected as a GA representative to the Continental Congress. He died from a serious leg wound that he sustained in a duel of pistols with his political rival, Lachlan McIntosh, who is also buried in this cemetery.

 WALK NORTH ON ABERCORN STREET TO OGLETHORPE SQUARE.

OGLETHORPE SQUARE- This square was laid out in 1742 and was originally known as Upper New Square. It was later renamed in honor of James Edward Oglethorpe, the founder of Georgia.

30 OWENS-THOMAS HOUSE- (c1819) This English Regency style home was originally built for Richard Richardson, a cotton broker, who lost the home due to financial problems only 3 years after it was completed. It was the first of many prominent homes to be designed by architect William Jay who was 23 years old at the time. George Owens purchased the home in 1830 and it remained in his family until his granddaughter, Margaret Thomas, willed it to the Telfair Museum of Art in 1951. The Marquis de Lafayette, a wealthy French citizen and soldier who greatly assisted the Americans during the Revolutionary War, visited Savannah in 1825 to dedicate the Nathanael Greene Monument (see 1). He stayed at this house during his visit and addressed the people of Savannah from the southern balcony facing President Street.

 WALK EAST ON PRESIDENT STREET TO COLUMBIA SQUARE.

COLUMBIA SQUARE- This square was laid out in 1799 and was named after Columbia, the goddess-like national personification of the United States.

31 KEHOE HOUSE- (c1892) William Kehoe was a poor Irish immigrant who worked his way up from being an apprentice in an iron foundry to becoming one of Savannah's most successful businessmen. This building was originally constructed as a residence for Mr. and Mrs. Kehoe and their 10 children. The Kehoe heirs sold the home in 1930 and it has since been a boarding house and a funeral parlor. It is now a fine inn. Rumors persist that the inn is haunted by two Kehoe twins that died while playing in one of the home's chimneys.

◄ This is a photo (c1890's) of the Kehoe Iron Works Foundry. Although terribly dilapidated, the foundry is still standing near the south end of Trustee's Garden (see 11).

32 DAVENPORT HOUSE MUSEUM- (c1820) This Federal-style home was built by master-builder Isaiah Davenport as his family residence and a showplace of his fine craftsmanship. By the early 20th century the home had become a tenement housing as many as 10 families. It was slated to be demolished in 1955 to make room for a parking lot. However, a group of seven determined civic-minded ladies formed the Historic Savannah Foundation which purchased the home for $22,500 and saved it from destruction.

WALK WEST ON STATE STREET TO ABERCORN STREET. TURN RIGHT AND WALK NORTH ON ABERCORN STREET TO REYNOLDS SQUARE.

REYNOLDS SQUARE- This square was laid out in 1734 and was originally named Lower New Square. It was later renamed in honor of Georgia's first Royal Governor, John Reynolds.

33 JOHN WESLEY MONUMENT- (ERECTED 1969) This bronze statue of the founder of Methodism features a young John Wesley in Church of England vestments extending his right hand in love, exhortation and invitation while holding the Bible in his left. Wesley and his brother Charles arrived in Savannah in 1736 after Oglethorpe had requested that he serve as the minister of Christ Church (see). He is credited with starting the first protestant Sunday School and compiling the first hymnal used in Georgia. However, Wesley had a rough time while in the colony. He angered Oglethorpe and the trustees by preaching to the Indians and he also became enamored with a young lady that ended up marrying another man. After he refused to give her communion, her husband sued Wesley for defamation of character. After only a year and nine months in the colony, he quietly left town and returned to England.

34 THE FILATURE- Now occupied by a law firm, this trust lot is the former site of the Filature. This large barnlike structure was erected in 1751 for the purpose of reeling and weaving silk, a commodity that was intended to be exported to England. When the silk industry failed, the building was converted to an assembly and dance hall. It served as the city's primary government building until 1812 when the government offices were moved to the City Exchange (see). During his visit of 1791, President George Washington attended a grand ball held here in his honor.

35 THE PINK HOUSE- (c1789) Now a popular restaurant, it was originally built as the residence of James Habersham, Jr. who is rumored to haunt the place. It takes its name from the pink stucco that covers its antique bricks. It avoided the great fire of 1796 and during its long history it has served as a bank, a tea room and the headquarters of one of Sherman's generals.

 THIS IS THE END OF TOUR 2

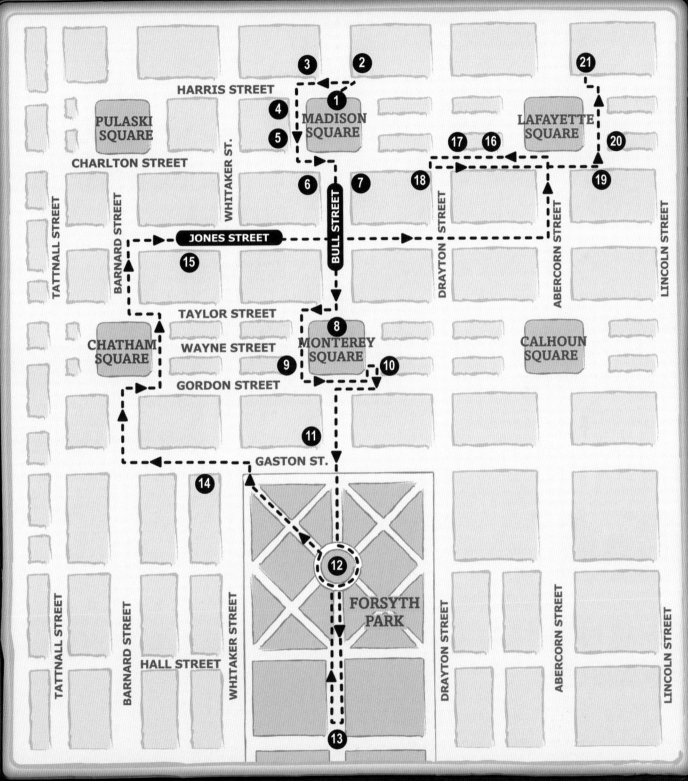

HARRIS STREET

PULASKI SQUARE

CHARLTON STREET

MADISON SQUARE

LAFAYETTE SQUARE

WHITAKER ST.

TATTNALL STREET

BARNARD STREET

JONES STREET

BULL STREET

DRAYTON STREET

ABERCORN STREET

LINCOLN STREET

TAYLOR STREET

CHATHAM SQUARE

WAYNE STREET

MONTEREY SQUARE

CALHOUN SQUARE

GORDON STREET

GASTON ST.

FORSYTH PARK

TATTNALL STREET

BARNARD STREET

HALL STREET

WHITAKER STREET

DRAYTON STREET

ABERCORN STREET

LINCOLN STREET

Walking time: approx. 1 hour · Walking distance: approx. 1.5 miles

N
W E
S

TOUR 3

MADISON SQUARE- Laid out in 1837, this square was named in honor of James Madison, the fourth President of the United States

1 SERGEANT JASPER MONUMENT- This bronze statue honoring William Jasper was completed in 1888. Jasper was a Revolutionary hero from South Carolina who first earned distinction at the Battle of Sullivan's Island in Charleston. Ignoring heavy fire from the British fleet, he re-raised the American battle flag that had been shot down. This rallied the Americans to continue fighting and the British were defeated. During the Siege of Savannah in 1779, Jasper again tried to rally his fellow soldiers by raising their flag under heavy fire but this time he was shot and killed. (see 2)

▲ Jasper raising the flag at the Spring Hill Redoubt during the Siege of Savannah.

2 DESOTO HILTON- This site was previously occupied by the Hotel Desoto which opened in 1890. During its time, it was a grand hotel that rivaled the finest hotels in New York and Florida. It was a Romanesque style building designed by William Preston, who also designed the Cotton Exchange (see 5), the Old Chatham County Courthouse (see 19) and the Savannah Volunteer Guards Armory (see 7). It was torn down in 1966 and was replaced by the current Desoto Hilton Hotel.

"Fireproof, And It's Famous" A catchy slogan in 1931.
▼

3 THE OLD SORREL-WEED HOUSE (c1841) Considered one of the finest examples of Greek Revival-Regency architecture in Savannah, this home was originally built for Francis Sorrel, a shipping merchant. It was sold to Henry Weed in 1859. This home was a social hotspot during the 1840's-50's and many prominent people were entertained here including General Robert E. Lee.

4 GREEN-MELDRIM HOUSE (c1853) This Gothic Revival home was originally built for Charles Green, an Englishman who was a wealthy cotton merchant. When Savannah was surrendered to the Union Army in December 1864, Green offered his home to General Sherman to serve as his headquarters while in Savannah. It was from here that Sherman sent his famous telegram to President Lincoln presenting the city as a Christmas gift. The home was later occupied by the Meldrim family who sold the home in 1943 to St. John's Episcopal Church to be used as a parish house.

◀ The man that spared Savannah, Major General William Tecumseh Sherman (c May 1865).

▲ General Sherman's Christmas Dinner at the Green's.

5 ST. JOHN'S CHURCH- Chartered as an expansion parish to Christ Church (see ③) in 1841, this building was built in 1853 and is known for its beautiful sounding bell chimes.

6 GRYPHON TEA ROOM- This unusual building was built as the Scottish Rite Temple in 1912. It is now operated by SCAD as the Gryphon Tea Room. The ground floor was once occupied by Solomon's Drug Store, one of the oldest pharmacies in the country.

7 SCAD- POETTER HALL (c1893) Originally constructed as the Savannah Volunteer Guards Armory, this is the first building that was purchased and renovated by the Savannah College of Art and Design or "SCAD." The school opened in this building in 1979. It is now known as Poetter Hall in honor of May and Paul Poetter who co-founded SCAD with Richard Rowan and Paula Wallace, the current president of the school. SCAD has contributed greatly to the preservation of historic Savannah and now occupies over 60 buildings in the area.

  WALK SOUTH ON BULL STREET TO MONTEREY SQUARE.

MONTEREY SQUARE- Commemorating the Battle of Monterey where American forces captured the Mexican city of Monterey during the Mexican-American War, this square was laid out in 1847. It is considered by many Savannahians to be the most luxurious square in town.

8 PULASKI MONUMENT (c1852) Casimir Pulaski was a skilled Polish soldier who is known as "the father of American cavalry." He was exiled from Poland after rebelling against Russian rule. Benjamin Franklin recommended that General George Washington accept Pulaski as a volunteer. In a letter to Washington penned shortly after arriving in America, Pulaski wrote "I came here, where freedom is being defended, to serve it, and to live or die for it." Pulaski's cavalry charge at the Battle of Brandywine is credited with saving Washington's life. Pulaski died as a result of infection from a grapeshot wound suffered during the Siege of Savannah in 1779. (see ②)

It is believed that the remains interred underneath this monument are Pulaski's. In 1852 and 1996 respectively, ▲ groups of doctors determined that the remains are consistent with the known features of Pulaski. The group from 1996 hoped to prove his identity by DNA evidence but was unsuccessful due to 200+ years of deterioration.

9 MERCER-WILLIAMS HOUSE- Construction of this home for General Hugh Mercer began in 1860 but was interrupted by the Civil War. It was completed in 1868, but Mercer never occupied the home. Jim Williams, a Savannah preservationist, purchased the home in 1969. The book, Midnight in the Garden of Good and Evil, made this home a landmark. It was in the study of this home that the alleged murder of Danny Hansford occurred. Williams was ultimately found not guilty after his fourth trial.

10 TEMPLE MICKVE ISRAEL (c1878) About 5 months after Oglethorpe's original landing, a group of 42 Jews from London arrived by ship in Savannah. They immediately formed a congregation which is now considered the third oldest Jewish congregation in America. This is the only Gothic style synagogue in America.

◄ As seen in this photo from 1920, the adjacent trust lot was once occupied by First Presbyterian Church which was also a Gothic style house of worship. The church was later demolished to make way for a science building for Armstrong College.

TOUR 3

WALK SOUTH ON BULL STREET TOWARD FORSYTH PARK.

11 THE ARMSTRONG MANSION (c1919) Now serving as a law office, this grand Italian Renaissance style mansion was built for George Armstrong, a successful shipping businessman. In 1935, Armstrong's widow gave the home to the City of Savannah to serve as a junior college. Now known as Armstrong Atlantic University, it moved to the south side of town in 1966.

FORSYTH PARK- Originally established in the 1840s on 10 acres of land donated by William Hodgson, the park was expanded by 20 acres and renamed in honor of Georgia Governor John Forsyth in 1851. This large park was anticipated by Oglethorpe's plan and was once the southern edge of town. Throughout its history it has served as a location for large public events and celebrations.

12 FORSYTH FOUNTAIN- Erected in 1858, this gorgeous cast iron fountain is probably the most photographed site in Savannah. Similar fountains exist in Cuzco, Peru and Poughkeepsie, NY and all are thought to be patterned after the fountain in Paris's Place de la Concorde. The fountain has undergone extensive renovations throughout the years with the last major effort occurring in 1988.

13 CONFEDERATE MONUMENT- Erected in 1874 in honor of Confederate soldiers who died in the Civil War, this monument was made in Canada and transported to Savannah by ship so that it would never touch "Yankee" soil. A portion of Fort Sumter's flag (where the first shots of the war were fired) lies in the cornerstone. The Confederate soldier atop the monument faces toward his enemy in the North.

TURN AROUND AND WALK NORTH TO FORSYTH FOUNTAIN. THEN WALK NORTHWEST TOWARD THE INTER- SECTION OF GASTON STREET AND WHITAKER STREET.

14 GEORGIA HISTORICAL SOCIETY- HODGSON HALL (c1876) Built to house the Georgia His- torical Society which was established in 1839 by the state legislature, this hall was named in memory of William Brown Hodgson, a well known scholar who was married to Margaret Telfair. The hall is open to the public and contains a wealth of historical documents and artifacts per- taining to the history of Savannah and Georgia.

WALK WEST ON GASTON STREET TO BARNARD STREET. TURN RIGHT AND WALK NORTH ON BARNARD STREET THROUGH CHATHAM SQUARE AND CONTINUING TO JONES STREET. TURN RIGHT AND WALK EAST ON JONES STREET.

15 MRS. WILKES' DINING ROOM- In 1943, a young Sema Wilkes took over a boardinghouse in downtown Savannah with the modest goal of offering comfortable lodging and home-style southern cooking served family style in the downstairs dining room. Today, the boarders are no longer present but the dining room continues to thrive as a favorite dining experience of visitors and Savannahians alike.

 CONTINUE WALKING EAST ON JONES STREET TO ABERCORN STREET. TURN LEFT AND WALK NORTH ON ABERCORN STREET TO LAFAYETTE SQUARE.

LAFAYETTE SQUARE- Laid out in 1837, this square is named in honor of the Marquis de Lafayette, a wealthy French citizen and soldier who greatly assisted the Americans during the Revolutionary War.

◀ Early morning in Lafayette Square.

Marquis de ▶ Lafayette

TOUR 3

16 ANDREW LOW HOUSE- This home was built in 1849 for Andrew Low, a British cotton broker. He died in 1886, the same year that his son, William Mackay Low, married Juliette Gordon. William inherited the home from his father and the couple lived here when in Savannah. They spent most of their married life in Great Britain. Their marriage was an unhappy one and they were in the process of a divorce when William died suddenly in 1905. William left most of his substantial estate to his mistress. His American holdings including this home were left to Juliette and she lived here as a widow until her death in 1927. It was during this time that Juliette established the Girl Scouts of America.

17 GIRL SCOUT FIRST HEADQUARTERS- Located to the rear of the Andrew Low House, this carriage house once served as the First Headquarters for the Girl Scouts. While living in England in 1911, Juliette Gordon Low became acquainted with Sir Robert Baden-Powell, the founder of the Boy Scouts and Girl Guides. Juliette became particularly interested in this youth movement. She decided to 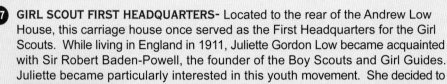 return to Savannah to start an organization in America. On March 12, 1912, she gathered 18 girls and held the first meeting of the American Girl Guides, later renamed the Girl Scouts. Upon her death in 1927, Juliette willed the carriage house to the Girl Scouts. It is now open to the public as a museum. Juliette Low (right) with Troop 1 ▶

18 LOUISA PORTER HOME- LOCATION OF THE FIRST GIRL SCOUT MEETING- The actual first meeting of the American Girl Guides on March 12, 1912 took place in this home that was once located across Drayton Street from the Girl Scout First Headquarters. At the first meeting Juliette established the first two troops known as the White Rose and Carnation patrols. Juliette's niece, Daisy Gordon, was the first registered member of the new group. The Louisa Porter Home was later demolished to make way for the office building that now occupies the lot.

▲ Louisa Porter Home

19 FLANNERY O'CONNOR HOUSE- This was the childhood home of Flannery O' Connor, an important American author with a flair for writing stories in the "Southern Gothic" style. It is known that her experiences in this home, just steps away from the Cathedral of St. John the Baptist, played a large part in her writing. Much of it reflected her Catholic faith and involved questions of morality and ethics. Unfortunately, she died from lupus at the young age of 39.

20 HAMILTON-TURNER HOUSE (c1873) Now a fine inn, this mansion was built for former Mayor and successful jeweler Samuel Pugh Hamilton and his wife Sara Hamilton. It was the first home in Savannah to feature electric lights. It was also a social center for Savannah's elite in its early days. In Midnight in the Garden of Good and Evil, it was featured as the party hotspot known as Mandy's Place. Rumors persist that Mr. Hamilton and his children still make frequent surprise visits.

21 CATHEDRAL OF ST. JOHN THE BAPTIST- The colonial charter of Savannah prohibited Catholics from settling in Savannah. The English Trustees feared that Catholics would be more loyal to the Spanish in Florida than the English. This prohibition faded shortly after the Revolutionary War and this congregation was organized around 1796. Construction began on this awe-inspiring cathedral in 1873 and was completed by the addition of the spires in 1896. It was almost totally destroyed by fire in 1898 and through diligent efforts was rebuilt by 1899. Today the Diocese of Savannah includes 90 counties in southern Georgia.

 THIS IS THE END OF TOUR 3.

This photo from 1893 shows the Cathedral prior to ▲ the spires being added and prior to the fire of 1898.

24

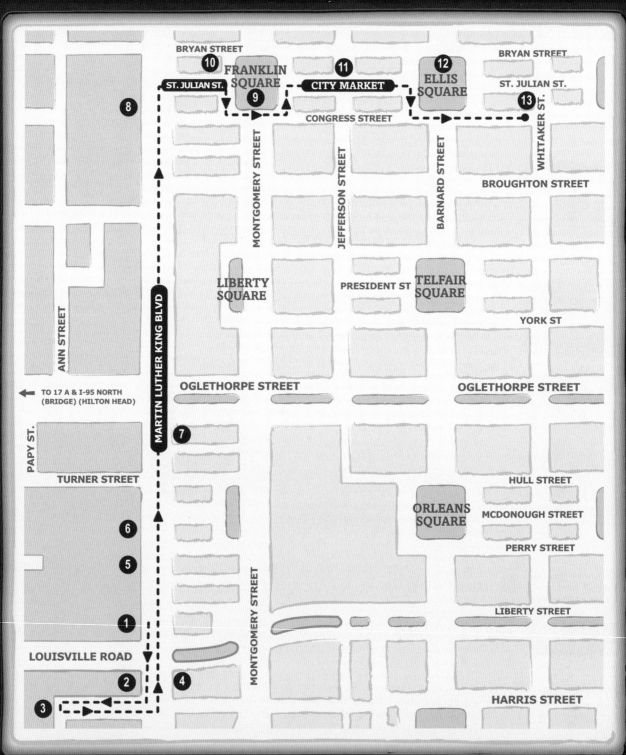

BRYAN STREET

⑩ FRANKLIN SQUARE

ST. JULIAN ST.

⑨

CITY MARKET

BRYAN STREET

⑫ ELLIS SQUARE

ST. JULIAN ST.

⑬

⑧

CONGRESS STREET

MONTGOMERY STREET

JEFFERSON STREET

BARNARD STREET

WHITAKER ST.

BROUGHTON STREET

LIBERTY SQUARE

PRESIDENT ST

TELFAIR SQUARE

YORK ST

MARTIN LUTHER KING BLVD

ANN STREET

TO 17 A & I-95 NORTH (BRIDGE) (HILTON HEAD)

OGLETHORPE STREET

OGLETHORPE STREET

PAPY ST.

⑦

HULL STREET

TURNER STREET

ORLEANS SQUARE

MCDONOUGH STREET

⑥

PERRY STREET

⑤

MONTGOMERY STREET

①

LIBERTY STREET

LOUISVILLE ROAD

② ④

HARRIS STREET

③

Walking time: approx. 35 minutes • Walking distance: approx. .8 miles

1 SAVANNAH VISITOR INFORMATION CENTER & SAVANNAH HISTORY MUSEUM (c1861) This building previously served as the passenger terminal for the Central Railroad and Banking Company of Georgia (later Central of Georgia Railway). The last passenger train departed from here in 1971. The Railroad also operated buildings to the north and south of this terminal. Any visitor to Savannah should stop here. Friendly greeters will provide information about all things of interest in Savannah. In addition, there are gift shops and theatres showing history films of Savannah. The Museum contains many items of interest including a classic Central of Georgia Locomotive, a working cotton gin, a replica of the "Bird Girl" statue and the actual bench used in the movie Forrest Gump.

SAVANNAH HISTORY MUSEUM ▶

 WALK SOUTH ON MARTIN LUTHER KING JR. BLVD. ACROSS LOUISVILLE ROAD.

2 BATTLEFIELD MEMORIAL PARK- This memorial is a replica of the Spring Hill Redoubt that was the center of fighting during the Revolutionary War's "Siege of Savannah." The actual location of this redoubt is a little further west of this location but the battle occurred all around this area. In the early morning hours of October 9, 1779, a combined French and American force of approximately 5,500 troops launched a disorganized attack to take back Savannah from the British. The British force of about 2,500 troops was entrenched and prepared to defend the city. It is believed that the British had advance knowledge of where the Franco-Americans intended to attack. In about one hour the second bloodiest battle of the Revolutionary War was over and the British were the decisive victors. The Franco Americans lost between 600-1,000 men and the British lost only 18. William Jasper (see ❶) and Casimir Pulaski (see ❽) were among those patriots who fought and died here.

◀ **SIEGE OF SAVANNAH** Fighting at the Spring Hill Redoubt, October 9, 1779

3 ROUNDHOUSE RAILROAD MUSEUM- A favorite for kids of all ages, this museum features a large collection of historic locomotives and rolling stock. This massive facility, constructed in 1835, served as a train construction and repair facility for the Central of Georgia Railway. It is a part of the most complete antebellum railroad complex in the United States. Today, you can ride on a train and take a spin on the large turntable.

 TURN AROUND AND WALK BACK NORTH ON MARTIN LUTHER KING JR. BLVD. TO THE INTERSECTION OF MLK AND LIBERTY STREET/LOUISVILLE ROAD.

4 MARRIOTT COURTYARD HOTEL- This hotel and the surrounding property were formerly the home of St. Patrick's Catholic Church.

◀ **ST. PATRICK'S CATHOLIC CHURCH-** Established as the second Catholic parish in Savannah after St. John's, this parish was organized in 1865 and the large Romanesque church was completed in 1879. During its time, West Broad Street (now Martin Luther King Jr. Blvd.) at Liberty Street was a significant commercial intersection. So prized was its real estate that the church was torn down in 1941 to make way for commercial development.

▲ This photo from 1919 of the intersection of MLK Blvd. and Liberty Street shows the commercial vibrancy of this corridor. Unfortunately, the construction of I-16 in the 1960's destroyed numerous buildings (including Union Station) and bisected the neighborhood which led to a general decline of business activity in this area.

CONTINUE WALKING NORTH ON MARTIN LUTHER KING JR. BLVD.

5 THE RED BUILDING- EICHBERG HALL (c1887) This building originally served as a terminal and administrative offices for the Central of Georgia Railway. SCAD saved this building from demolition in 1988 when it purchased and renovated the building and terminal sheds to serve as the architecture, historic preservation, interior design and urban design departments of the school.

6 THE GRAY BUILDING- KIAH HALL- SCAD MUSEUM OF ART (c1856) This Greek Revival style building is the oldest surviving railroad office building in the United States. A Savannah Daily News story in 1859 called it "a marvel of solidity and beauty." It predates the Red Building and the passenger terminal where the Savannah Visitor Center is located. It served as the headquarters of the Central of Georgia Railway. SCAD renamed the building Kiah Hall in honor of African-American artist Virginia Jackson Kiah. Today it houses the SCAD Museum of Art (open to the public) and the Earle W. Newton Center for British and American Studies.

◀ This photo from around 1950 shows the entire Central of Georgia Railway complex.

7 BARCLAY-WETTER HOUSE- This desolate lot at the southeast corner of MLK and Oglethorpe Ave. is the home of a lost treasure of Savannah. Built originally in 1822 by Anthony Barclay, it was later purchased by Augustus Wetter who installed its famous ironwork in 1857. In 1950, the building was demolished in order to open a used car lot on the site. Prior to its destruction, the ironwork was auctioned off and some examples can be found in front of the Cotton Exchange(see 5) and the Philbrick-Eastman House(see 26) as well as around the Old Harbor Light(see 10) .

FORMER LOCATION BARCLAY-WETTER HOUSE

8 SHIPS OF THE SEA MUSEUM-SCARBROUGH HOUSE (c1819) This home was designed by William Jay and built for William Scarbrough, a successful shipping merchant who moved to Savannah in 1802. In 1818, he became the principal investor and president of the Savannah Steamship Company. The company built the steamship Savannah which became the first steamship to successfully cross the Atlantic in 1819. Unfortunately, the project was a money pit and it sunk the fortunes of many prominent Savannahians including Scarbrough who was declared insolvent in 1820. Now home to the Ships of the Sea Museum, it features a vast display of large model ships and all things nautical.

BARCLAY-WETTER HOUSE

▲ THE STEAMSHIP SAVANNAH

BARCLAY-WETTER HOUSE IRONWORK

TURN RIGHT AND WALK EAST ON W. ST. JULIAN STREET TO FRANKLIN SQUARE.

FRANKLIN SQUARE- This square was laid out in 1791 and was named in honor of Benjamin Franklin, the famous inventor and statesman. Franklin served as Georgia's colonial representative in London from 1768 to 1775.

This photo from 1890 shows why this square used to be known as Water Tower Square. ▶ This masonry tower rose 80 feet above the square and served as a reservoir for the early waterworks of the city. The large steeple of the First African Baptist Church (see 10) that was lost in the storm of 1893 is also visible in this photo.

27

9 HAITIAN MONUMENT (ERECTED 2007) This monument honors a group of 700 free men of color from the Island of Haiti who fought beside the Americans and French in the Siege of Savannah in 1779. This group was the largest unit of men of African descent to fight in the American Revolution.

10 FIRST AFRICAN BAPTIST (c1859) This church is the home of the oldest black congregation in America. Andrew Bryan, a former slave who had purchased his freedom, led the church to official recognition in 1788. This facility was constructed in the 1850s by free African-Americans and slaves who were allowed to work after their normal work day. It was a stop on the Underground Railroad for runaway slaves and the holes in the floorboards of the sanctuary served as air holes for those hiding underneath.

11 CITY MARKET- This is a great place to shop, take in some art, dine and relax. Today's city market is a collection of 4 buildings that house many shops, restaurants and art galleries. This location is not the City Market that the old time Savannahians remember. The Old City Market is the next stop on our tour.

  WALK EAST THROUGH CITY MARKET TO ELLIS SQUARE.

ELLIS SQUARE- This square was one of the original four laid out in 1733. It was named Ellis Square in honor of Henry Ellis, the second Royal Governor of Georgia. In 1763, the colonial legislature moved the public market from Wright Square to Ellis Square. This square has been commonly known as Market Square ever since. **ELLIS SQUARE RECONSTRUCTION 2009**

12 OLD CITY MARKET- Numerous market structures were built here over the years but the "Old City Market" building was completed in 1872. It served as a market until 1950 when it was demolished to make way for an awful looking parking deck. The loss of this treasure was the catalyst of organized historic preservation efforts in Savannah. The city ultimately reclaimed the site and completed a new interactive public square in 2010.

OLD CITY MARKET

OLD CITY MARKET INTERIOR

  WALK EAST ON W. CONGRESS STREET.

13 PAULA DEEN'S THE LADY AND SONS RESTAURANT- In 1989, Paula Deen started a lunch delivery service called "The Bag Lady" out of her home. The business grew and eventually became a full service restaurant known as "The Lady" which was located in the Best Western hotel on the Southside of town. The restaurant moved downtown in 1996 and was renamed "The Lady & Sons". It moved once more to its current location which opened in November 2003. If you are hungry for good southern home cooking, this is the place.

  THIS IS THE END OF TOUR 4.

SAVANNAH MEMORIES

This view north on Bull Street toward Johnson Square from the 1890's is the photo that inspired this book. I walk down this exact stretch of Bull Street between Congress and Broughton almost daily. This photo reminded me of the fact that I am treading over ground that is rich with interesting history every time I walk in downtown Savannah. It became my desire to share that realization with other Savannahians and visitors alike.

This photo of the castle-like Odd Fellows' Hall on Telfair Square (lost in Hogan's Fire of 1889) inspires me to remember Savannah's architectural treasures that were lost over the years to fires, natural disasters and wrecking balls. These memories foster a spirit of appreciation for the seven pioneering women who founded the Historic Savannah Foundation to protect and preserve Savannah's treasures.

This 1957 view of Johnson Square shows all three of the "skyscrapers" that were demolished to make way for the Suntrust building and parking deck. It serves as a recent reminder that Historic Savannah is a part of a dynamic city that will continue to change and evolve over time.

This fantastic shot of the Hotel Desoto from Madison Square is pictorial evidence that trees (namely Live Oaks) have changed the face of Savannah's squares significantly over time.

This photo (c 1893) of the main hall of The Savannah Cotton Exchange reminds me of the fine craftsmanship that exists inside many of the homes and buildings that we marvel at from the outside.

This is a photograph (c 1906) of Union Station, a magnificent train station that was demolished to make way for Interstate 16. It does not appear in the tours as it was just a little too far out of the way (located where I-16 crosses MLK). It is a great reminder that the sites in this book just scratch the surface of Savannah's rich history. There are many exciting places outside of Savannah's Historic District to visit and explore including Bonaventure Cemetery, Old Fort Jackson, Fort Pulaski, Isle of Hope, Wormsloe and many others.

ACKNOWLEDGEMENTS

I do not have enough space to individually thank everyone who assisted in my efforts to create this book so please consider this a big "Thank You!" to all involved. I would like to offer special thanks to the following people: Paula, my wonderful wife, and Cameron and Ethan, my two boys, who allowed me time to work on this project; My Mom for encouragement; Ben Edelstein, the designer who made the pages come to life; Brian and Allison, my brother and sister-in-law, who were my test walkers; Joe Rudzinskas, a good friend who allowed me to use his expensive camera; Clay Collins, a good friend to bounce ideas off of; Joe Marinelli, President of the Savannah Area Convention & Visitors Bureau, for his insight, assistance and encouragement.

In memory of my Dad,
a native Savannahian and a true Southern gentleman.

PHOTO CREDITS

Armstrong Atlantic University, Lane Library, Florence Powell Minis Collection- Multiple images- Artwork of Savannah, W.H. Parish Publishing co., 1893 - Special thanks to Caroline Hopkinson.

Central of Georgia Railway Historical Society, Inc.- Tour 4 Stop 6 - Aerial of Railroad Complex- Special thanks to Allen Tuten, President.

Coastal Heritage Society- www.chsgeorgia.org- Tour 4 Stop 1 -Savannah Visitor Information Center.

Georgia Historical Society- www.georgiahistory.com-Historic Drawings & Photos- View of Savannah 1734 pg 2, Naval Stores pg 3, Sherman Entering Savannah pg 5, Pontoon Bridge pg 5, Board of Trade pg 6, River Street 1900s pg 8, Waving Girl at Elba & Portrait pg 8, Johnson Square Bus. Ctr. pg 11, Gas Station pg 12, Germania Bank pg 12, Whitney Hotel pg 12, Liberty Bank pg 12, Broughton St pg 12, Liberty Pole pg 13, Old City Market pg 13, Odd Fellows' Hall & Fire pg 13,29, Tomochichi pg 15, Porter-Gilmer House pg 15, View on Bull pg 15, 1833 Courthouse pg 16, 1843 Lutheran Church pg 16, Savannah Theatre pg 17, Desoto Billboard pg 21, Christmas Dinner pg 21, Presbyterian Church pg 22, Louisa Porter Home pg 24, Street Scene pg 26, SS Savannah pg 27, Wetter House & Ironwork pg 27, Old City Market & Interior pg 28, View of Johnson Square pg 29, Hotel Desoto pg 30- Special thanks to Nora Lewis and Rana Edgar.

SavannahVisit.com- Cotton Exchange Griffon, cover, pg 1- Mercer-Williams House, cover, pg 1,22- Oglethorpe Monument, cover, pg 2,17- Lafayette Square, pg 23- River Street Aerial, pg 8 - Special thanks to the Savannah Area Convention & Visitors Bureau.

The New York Public Library- Tour 1 Stop 6, View of Factors Walk- Tour 1 Stop 8, City Exchange- Tour 2 Stop 2, Screven House- Tour 2 Stop 15, Burial Mound- Robert N. Dennis Collection of Stereoscopic Views, Miriam & Ira D. Wallach Division of Art, Prints & Photographs, The New York Public Library, Astor, Lenox and Tilden Foundations

Tour 3 Stop 1, Jasper Raising Flag- Emmet Collection, Miriam and Ira D. Wallach Division of Art, Prints and Photographs, The New York Library, Astor, Lenox and Tilden Foundations

INDEX
REFERENCED BY PAGE NUMBER

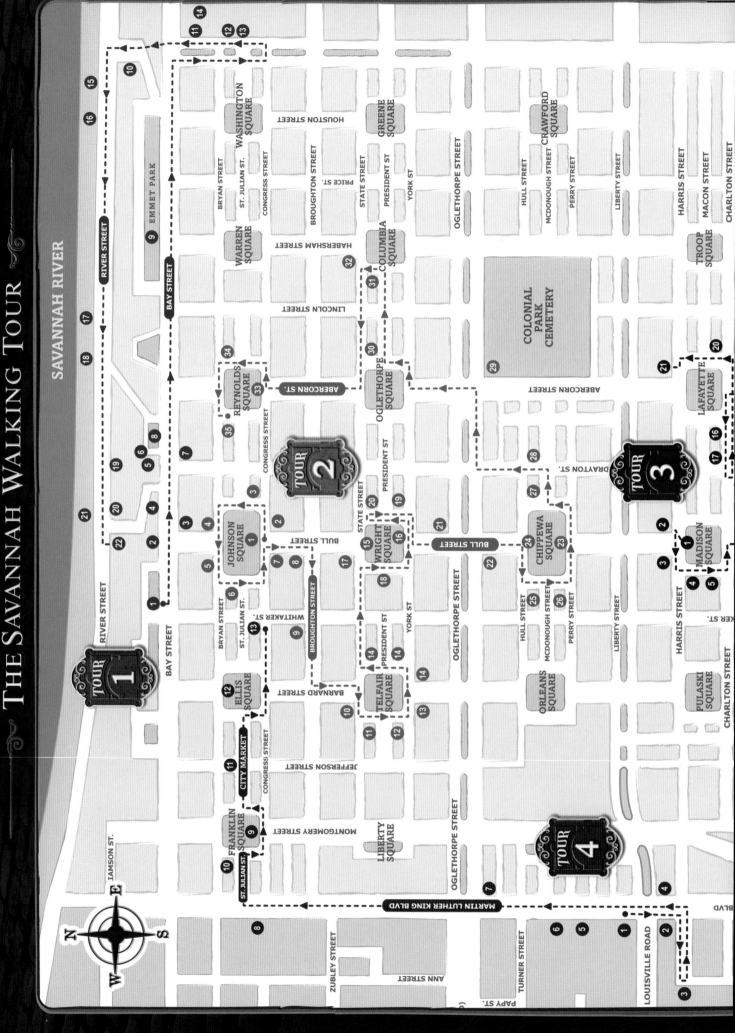

The Savannah Walking Tour

SAVANNAH RIVER